LIST

T0166427

ALSO BY NICOLE BROSSARD (IN TRANSLATION)

POETRY

Ardour (2015; translated by Angela Carr)

White Piano (2013; translated by Robert Majzels and Erín Moure)

Notebook of Roses and Civilization (2007; translated by Robert Majzels and Erín Moure)

Installations (2000; translated by Robert Majzels and Erín Moure)

Lovhers (1986; translated by Barbara Godard)

Daydream Mechanics (1980; translated by Larry Shouldice)

ESSAYS

Fluid Arguments (2005; edited by Susan Rudy, with new translations by Anne-Marie Wheeler)

She would be the first sentence of my next novel (1998; translated by Susanne de Lotbinière-Harwood)

The Aerial Letter (1988, 2020; translated by Marlene Wildeman)

ANTHOLOGIES

Avant Desire: A Nicole Brossard Reader (2020; edited by Sina Queyras, Geneviève Robichaud, and Erin Wunker)

Nicole Brossard: Selections (2010; edited by Jennifer Moxley)

Mobility of Light: The Poetry of Nicole Brossard (2009; edited by Louise Forsyth)

The Blue Books (2003; reissue of *A Book*, *Turn of a Pang*, and *French Kiss*)

FICTION

Fences in Breathing (2009; translated by Susanne de Lotbinière-Harwood)

Picture Theory (2006; translated by Barbara Godard)

Yesterday, at the Hotel Clarendon (2005; translated by Susanne de Lotbinière-Harwood)

Baroque at Dawn (1997; translated by Patricia Claxton)

Mauve Desert (1990, 2006, 2015; translated by Susanne de Lotbinière-Harwood)

Surfaces of Sense (1989; translated by Fiona Strachan)

French Kiss (1986; translated by Patricia Claxton)

These Our Mothers, or, The Disintegrating Chapter (1983; translated by Barbara Godard)

Turn of a Pang (1976; translated by Patricia Claxton)

A Book (1976; translated by Larry Shouldice)

PROSE

Intimate Journal (2004; translated by Barbara Godard)

MUSEUM OF BONE AND WATER

NICOLE BROSSARD

Translated by Robert Majzels and Erín Moure

First published in French in 1999 by Éditions du Noroît and Cadex Éditions
First published in English in 2003 by House of Anansi Press
This edition published in Canada in 2021 and the USA in 2021 by
House of Anansi Press Inc.
www.houseofanansi.com

House of Anansi Press is committed to protecting our natural environment. This book is made of material from well-managed FSC®-certified forests, recycled materials, and other controlled sources.

House of Anansi Press is a Global Certified Accessible™ (GCA by Benetech) publisher. The ebook version of this book meets stringent accessibility standards and is available to students and readers with print disabilities.

25 24 23 22 21 1 2 3 4 5

Library and Archives Canada Cataloguing in Publication

Title: Museum of bone and water / Nicole Brossard ; translated by Robert Majzels and Erín Moure. Other titles: Musée de l'os et de l'eau. English | Names: Brossard, Nicole, author. | Majzels, Robert, 1950– translator. | Mouré, Erin, 1955– translator.
Description: Previously published: Toronto, ON: Anansi, 2003. |
Translation of: Musée de l'os et de l'eau. | Poetry.
Identifiers: Canadiana (print) 20200198882 | Canadiana (ebook) 20200198912 |
ISBN 9781487008093 (softcover) | ISBN 9781487008109 (PDF)
Classification: LCC PS8503.R7 M8713 2021 | DDC C841/.914—dc23

Series design: Brian Morgan
Cover illustration: Mathilde Cinq-Mars

House of Anansi Press respectfully acknowledges that the land on which we operate is the Traditional Territory of many Nations, including the Anishinabeg, the Wendat, and the Haudenosaunee. It is also the Treaty Lands of the Mississaugas of the Credit.

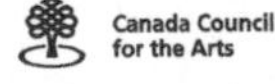

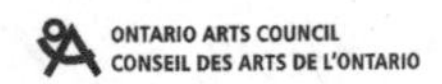

We acknowledge for their financial support of our publishing program the Canada Council for the Arts, the Ontario Arts Council, and the Government of Canada.

Printed and bound in Canada

CONTENTS

A Museum Contemporary in Time

A translators' introduction

ROBERT MAJZELS AND ERÍN MOURE

Nicole Brossard's *Museum of Bone and Water* is not a museum of mummified classification, nor a temple of forgotten culture, nor an institution of identity and exclusion. It is an exploded museum, fragmented, gathering disparate images, a museum for a time of shifting identities and meanings. Brossard's museum is a space of alterity. A museum in which she can imagine herself. And in which we, subsequently, can imagine both ourselves and each other, our relation.

Museum of Bone and Water is a manual for negotiating time, our time. It is contemporary and it is our contemporary.

It's not that some books age *better* than others, for books, once printed, remain the same. Their pages fade and go brittle, that's all. It's we, readers, who change. Curiously, any book we pick up and open, we can only read as contemporaries. We are contemporary always to the book in front of us, whether it is a tome by Seneca, by Virgil, by Zhuangzi, by Spinoza. The text before our eyes is received according to current conditions of reception. For literature is never just the printed volume of a text, it is a *third space*, that space between the printed volume and the reader, a space in continual regeneration.

For that reason, a translation of a book is never a reproduction of a printed text in another language, it is a reading, a projection of that third space between the printed volume and the reader who "translated" it. This projection too, again, once printed, awaits its reader. This is the contemporary, always, in literature.

Underlying every translation, of course, are the relations of power between the two languages, and translators of Nicole Brossard into English cannot ignore the Québécois struggle to preserve and vitalize French language and culture. As well, there are the relations of power between men and women, and the struggles for existence of gay and lesbian people, the struggle for recognition of sexuality's difference and splendour. At the heart of *our* translation, then, is a willingness to place ourselves at the service of Nicole Brossard's writing, and in her debt, by refusing to normalize her transgressive poetics. In our translation we carry her disruptive play into the English museum of language.

Of course, many translations, read by later contemporaries, suffer too much from their initial conditions of reception and become unreadable, in particular, as translations: Alexander Pope's *Iliad*, for example, reads today as so idiosyncratic to Pope that it is considered as part of Pope's literary output and not Homer's. When we want to read Homer "in English," it is not Pope that we reach for.

As such, whereas original books are often *footnoted* over time to maintain the guy wires of the contemporary, translations of books are *retranslated*.

Nicole Brossard's work, in *Museum of Bone and Water* and

elsewhere — for this book is but one talisman of her work, by one translating duo — is surprising in this context of thinking the contemporary: twenty years after its first appearance in the Majzels-Moure translation, it does not seem to need retranslation. It still meets us as contemporary to our thinking and concerns. In fact, in a way, it does something that goes beyond this meeting; it contemporizes its readers. Its bone and water will us continually and now into a contemporary space. This *Museum* almost creates its own conditions of reception, and doubly, for it is not simply Brossard but an acute reading of Brossard's original text: every word of the text in this book was written by Majzels and Moure reading Brossard.

For Nicole Brossard, in any case, all writing is already a translation, the translation of her experience and existence in the world into a language that she is compelled to splinter, disassemble, and reassemble in order to create a space for herself, for women writing, for lesbian desire.

It's a beautiful, sonorous text, and reveals some of what may be essential characteristics of Brossard's work in poetry (and her work in poetry underpins all her work in prose, if we may dare to say so): her syntactic shifts and doublings that create, to borrow a word used often by poet Chantal Neveu in the context of her own work, a *polysemy*. A multiplicity of tiny meaning-shifts and doubled presences that are actualized, made present, when and as we read.

In French, the title is *Musée de l'os et de l'eau*, visibly and aurally singular in construction; in English, the title could be single or plural in reference as *bone* is the general, *water* the general, singular and plural at once. Imagine if the French were made plural, you'd have *Musée des os et des eaux*, which would be almost a sonorous repetition . . . *dez o et dez o*, for the "s" in "os" is not pronounced in the plural word. Further, alert to the sonority of language to which Brossard is continually attentive, notice how *l'os* in the original is a homophone for the English word *loss*.

The act of translating requires us to pay close attention to the way that syntax, sound, and sight create meaning in a text. We move back and forth in the text as we work, rethinking and revising as we slowly build the version in English, so that the motion of reading is looping, skipping back and forward, at times excruciatingly slow, then suddenly flashing ahead. It is musical, because these poems are a fugue, a repetition accumulating difference, music to accompany a dance across the page — *brisé, chassé, cabriolé.* This being so, our work in translating *Museum of Bone and Water* was an ideal way for us to read, deeply and fully, *Musée de l'os et de l'eau.* For Brossard, time neither stands still nor advances in a plodding linear movement towards a better or more dismal future (depending on one's temperament and circumstance). Rather, time is a continuous doubling back and leaping sometimes forward, sometimes sideways, sometimes in place.

What distinguishes Brossard's writing practice from so much literature, whether past or contemporary, is its conscious abandoning of control over meaning, its invitation to the reader to share the work of making meaning. It is a testament to her generosity to readers and to translators, her relinquishing of the power of writer over text and over reader.

The experience of translating Nicole Brossard is equally one of generosity and one of disassembling power. As reader-translators, we write in service to the text in another language, to our target language, to each other—because we are reading together—to the "author," and to the reader, in a complex matrix of moving parts. The resulting translation is also still moving, shifting each time a reader engages with it.

Museum of Bone and Water traces our presences as solidities (bones) and liquidities (water). It engages our physical or somatic substrates, our relation to the world and to others, to one another, as well as to pain, anguish, and hope, their psychic substrates, and to breathing itself, in its very cadences.

Above all, though, when readers open it today, *Museum of Bone and Water* makes us its contemporary, as it did to the readers who first opened it in French in 1999 and in English in 2003.

MUSEUM OF BONE AND WATER

I know this by the words I am missing
my life has gone to sleep
in the contour so precise
of the tip of a long bone
though I still know how to smile
before Roman cloisters and their ossuaries
the value of *I love you*

1.

cold luminous November morning
I count my words
the bone that will not counter time

from the other side of silence
the art of peoples and of bones entangled

my answer never differs
water a way of hiding pain

2.

in Palermo the slow fall of ochre time
between my lips a threaded baroque yes I want
slow morning's procession

an arm of the sea and of the future
water that grips births

against all the squadrons
water as far as the eye can see abrading silence

3.

in Dresden a morning of station soot and museum
I stopped short at a map
index finger jabbed into destruction

welter of peoples and skulls
mass of marble and silence in the midst

no one will revive for tomorrow
to take up the conversation where it left off

4.

in San Cristóbal de las Casas a morning of
Black Virgin
of Coca-Cola and incense *siempre*
I caress an idea of life in the dust

smell of flesh and silence
red everywhere seeped into fabric

by dint of images flashes of fear
amor that chases off the goats

5.

water returns smell of glacier at my wrist
my museum life files past
head here chest there a harrowing work

in the distance Madrid shines beneath etchings of Goya
at the bottom of a page a detail of the *Cannibals* kills me

in the no-noise of knowledge
water all water I want it glacial

6.

morning or noon in the city I write
my head resting on humankind
and others too in repetition

on the line of the horizon as on the screen
we tear the alphabet from dawn's arms

hands, heart and muscles in the rain
detached from reality by brilliant procedures

7.

this morning not fretting about shade
I gather bones shells present of lavender
noble back visible far-off like bay water

all round the tongue cuts every rosebush
no one dares laugh once cleansed of it all

suspicion naturally a bone
art spies on art and my life

8.

May morning Ontario Street I observe
the bone and blue of questions
brush up against territory of when I was young

a theory of vanishing in mind
in each phrase the background murmur of farewell

thus tomorrow contemplated in tears
white thighs washed in river water

9.

silence between rosebushes flash indigo
I get used to questions to their shadow
in the bay of Palermo immediately thirst

nothing more troubled and bowed than the skull
the mouth having struggled for breath

the idea of carnage and vermilion
in my chest to the point of exhaustion

10.

always this mad trap of perception if
with Greek voice and a bit of chalk
I touch to the quick the morning languid with dew

bits of rejoinder and paper
in another life of tragedy I move with water

tell me what you intend with
the architecture of bodies and water all down their cheeks

11.

my joy in fiction engages every subject
suppose I've a body a skeleton sexed
a touch away from intimate words and self-portrait

in Dresden a morning of soot and frost
I cross the black and the white of three postcards

the ruined facade of the women's church
unimaginable gust of wind at my back

12.

the etchings of Goya in Madrid
crosshatch of bars convents ripple of cars
dancing in the dark at high noon

child's fingers caught between vowels
and the wool of prayer mats and luxury

simplicity of the verb
to die and its ink

13.

mere steps from the Voyageur bus depot the Taj Mahal
in the bent whiteness of noon
river water I caress your thighs

muscles myths that help me measure
the density of a shudder's water

the clear-cut hem of silence under your nails
the lapidary light

14.

red or blue a war has colour
of large shawls over women's shoulders
chickens and dogs enter the church

this morning will we dry out
truth like a pelt in the dust

San Cristóbal de las Casas smell of chewing gum
leather laces wooden crosses standing I drift

15.

every morning the slave absorbs the morning
without touching without licking from the soul's tip
water the strong odour of *The Odyssey*

my eyes are slow to pick out
god the heroes the last ship

the small boats their tortoiseshell gleam
from dawn to dark the same boats tilted

16.

the continuity of mornings of genesis
in rose-pink and nostalgia for the concrete: astonishment
    that obsesses
the joints. Knowledge holds fast flexible

gripped in the museum silence art of slow steps
it all moves so suddenly from sex to cortex

the love of lives and cities lodged in the pattern of bone
I must document my joy my shadow

17.

in the morning air don't be afraid
every surface is real
curving patterns and waterfalls

the rain a rainbow
back-to-back don't be afraid

height of *soledad* and splendour I want
to immolate my joy my shadow

18.

now I apportion the clamour of reds
at the end of each time a life
I document the abandonment the inundated dream

years of sleet and soot
I still have the same version: bone light on the knife

an animal's shudder. Paper crumpled
ink soaked up. Words of the era whispered in the dark

19.

I'd have liked us to talk a while longer
but of words too at the peak of their perfection
their fall from the midst of mirrors

and of the crowd shoulders stuck to the planets
of the finger pointing out the word *war* between bookshelves

and horizon. All that counts
the choice of caresses from ankle to wrists

20.

ever since the crumpling of landscapes
each tree and the morning quiver like long lashes
I never tire of the necessary appearance of the world

the value of *I love you* in each era
and silence. The skilled slowness of lips

on the young *female libido*. And the body
that bends so well beneath the future and so much water

THEATRE: SPEED OF WATER

water idea of water caressed
we often repeat
the same signs while touching
the depths of thought
skin laughing saline

yet we must bring silence back
to the start of the phrase to rally
plans of vertigo and exhilaration
for desire at arm's length
plunges us quickly amid
the sea already blue already drowned

a dark wind struck
yes among the forms
virtual to cut short the breath
the wind often raises
a thirst for words and questions
on each side of the dream
we astonish the thoughtful we

under the pressure of water
the idea the whole idea of shadow in us
the current of thoughts came after
so intimate so fragile the enamel of day-to-day
a bath of light a game
of shadows and mores
under the pressure of words

for a long time in separating
the peaks of waves I touched
the water of rapture
the liquid coating of the night

nothing gentles the world
there are words that disappear
taken back by the sea and its folds
a fecund architecture
while drawn close to our lips
intrigued by the tide
black
night brandishes its echo

the horizon draws from us
its colour and the breadth of dream
the world must reply
to the face we offer
unfathomable mouth

our lives are thus worn round
for eternity with sighs
and huge pebbles monstrous swallowing
the present so naturally
while we observe
a watch on our wrist
the pulse of our veins

what speaking signifies
still
when our hands insist
above the fractal chaos

our eyes affixed on the horizon
endlessly there are patterns
in our fecund lives
to repeat

our eyelids at night
if chaos files past in silence
our eyelids accept
the mystery

I'm expecting words
of extreme joy unstable
at the end of our appearance
there where we seek
to protect the species

nothing is missing
fiction strikes permanently
at full throttle
vague dimension of the future run out
elsewhere and immense
chance in our eyes
blue triumph

the universe is on the page one page
over
as dawn erases night
water has washed the sky and we said
the ink fled carrying with it
husks and antennae
the whole system of reproduction
the nudity of reasoning beings

FIGURE OF THE SLAVE
(Carnation)

1.

all night long the light will have changed
everywhere the bridges hemmed in blue
how to hold back the water
reality without placing myself in its midst

I slide my hand until dawn

2.

on the skin its surface I displace
grief and my questions the shivers
an idea
three-quarters of a silence upon a wound

sum of beings on a background of vile red

3.

life settles in implausible
immaterial you might say an invention
then morning of arrows and nudity
the flesh strums

on the tip of the tongue a dragon keeps vigil

4.

rose-pink immense deep in the eyes
the slave holds at her back
her hand her shadow years of rings
through which brief morning passes right to the bone

the soul of the slave goes nowhere

5.

unable to recapitulate the slave wanders
dust and sperm in her teeth
her hair a mess tradition what do I know
or the globalization of male vitalia

rumour runs in the mouth of the slave

6.

defiance: from the throat a sign
of a broad and firm no
then seeking a breach among the words
rose that curls furiously every petal

eyes of buffalo and children upon departing the city

7.

silence did we say how far
to get to the depth of the eye's water
of thirst and self
if the colour of fish if exhilaration triumph

raw passion that unsettles knowledge

8.

each month the slave counts
her egg the blows and the planets
lifts dust and the sheets
does not invent war

already blue vacillates all around

9.

the bulk of the precious world glitters
water *agua wasser eau aqua*
before the screens we recapitulate
planet in sight *la chair et la chair encore*

thousands of lips split in the brazen light don't you know

10.

in nature we've cut up
the world and answers
exposed the slave to all kinds of pain
to the reproduction of the small silences of death

of gold the slave's laugh created the worst of confusions

11.

intimacy torn out like a word from the dictionary
the slave holds fast everywhere
hands like sponges fascinated by the sea
she palpates the future

the coming traffic in souls and organs

12.

imagine all this that can't be put away
with facility fig figure
such a long time since you stopped touching
lies and so many other bones

up close you play constantly you snaffle up pleasure

TYPHOON THRUM

and it takes flight whitecaps typhoon thrum
like an elbow in the night
ray of mores
the world is swiftly dark

everywhere where the mouth is eccentric
it's snowing: and yet this heat long
beneath the tongue, the me curls up emotion
glides ribbon of joy
harmonic eyelids

as the world is swiftly dark
and night turns me avid
from everywhere so much brushes up
that the tongue with its salt
pierces one by one the words
with silence, typhoon thrum

in full flight if I spread my arms
my hair slow in the oxygen
I claim there are vast laws
beyond cities and sepultures
voice ribbon, eyes' blade

tonight if you lean your face close
and civilization stretches out
at the end of your arms, tonight
if in full flight you catch my image
say it was from afar
like a die in the night

and while my sex dreams of daybreak
engorges ecstatic epitheliums
it's snowing and again proximity
I claim it's the aura
or the image asymmetric
of the image in brief full flight

groundswell, image ceremony
my heart is agile
emotion between us
matter of laughter matter too true
and my voice that cracks
in the cold of galaxies

I claim I keep watch in silence
in the rose cold of galaxies
I claim that if the eye is black
it cannot keep watch

everywhere where the laughing virtual mouth
of energy devours dawn disgorges its yes
she cries out as wildly as she comes
tympanum, sonorous mauve
vast laws that lick
the air's depth from afar

in the morning the she glides high
and rivers beneath my skin
are long from so many windings
savoury with women and lucidity
in the morning the river surges swept away
when I touch you
face-to-face in affirmation

PALM TREES

THE PRESENT IS NOT A BOOK

because of the body the present
every day
landscapes at that place in my eyes
where women and other women touch
memory and pleasure

because of hands
of the line of time that runs through our hair
most of us dedicate our poems
life to girls capable of tongues and future

amid mirrors and screens
a way to approach silence
palm trees of Dublin or Key West
and other images where the rain seems infinite
a care for water that feels good
as life because of the body seeks
conversation others say culture here

because of words gone off on the Web
of life in the month of June that watches over
the present from one shore to the other
the palm trees on the Isle of Man
dogs haunted like museum prose
I squint my eyes wisely
to the best of my knowledge
I observe why everywhere

ideas are dying head-on
in our topical faces
our bodies personalized like perfumes
yet in the here and now
palm trees remain in the night
inexhaustibly green
so languorous that no question

because of the body the meaning of life
constantly changes vertigo
for if the ocean were at the far end of destiny
spark of green
delicate work of presence
intended for a nomad humanity
the future and the future would run together

yet the present comes swiftly
with each phrase a new configuration
of meaning where no one hesitates
in thought in rapture
the present is not a book
joy that traverses the rosebushes

THE EYES OF WOOLF AND BORGES

I can't seem to erase
the idea that faced with time
leaf or child
time repeats tempest
or labyrinth
no one dreams of resisting

of life we'll say any old thing in short
to save time *quick-*
cut: confusion of flash fool furious
sleep time of screens
real time of tête-à-tête and intimate talk
side-by-side spoken clearly
snippet of sincerity

we are predictable beings
summer we caress from afar
with our eyes the future in segments
the tongue in the mouth
mobile landscape
viable or vital
the cheekbone is soft
leaf or chalk

it's in the curve of the back
in the curve of women's bellies
the hand measures
time the simple need to compare
ex aequo long ago
fiction inveterate and a good-looking elsewhere
leaf or child
the heat once more of mouths
girl or leaf
the sentiment of so often

maybe we need a small incision
in silence with a fingernail
so that time mounts maternal
up to our temples the to-and-fro of memory
life caught in the fist like light

time sudden as if already
it no longer existed
from one end of this poem to the other
between each flutter of the heart
gone soft like the aftermath of love
or fraction of a second that frightens the athlete

in the books of Woolf and Borges
the time of the blind
the time of the woman with a thousand points of view
fine fluidity that hinders neither stone nor sea

if time swallowed suddenly
the view across dawn and my past
I would spend hours enrapt
in library or garden
in the reflection of every spine
ink and the vast vocabulary of existing

in the books of Woolf and Borges
a flutter of eyelashes
between London and Buenos Aires
a girl of thirteen with round glasses might wonder
how to let a city enter
the room in which she writes
where to make civilization begin
the speech of water the vertiginous number

KEY WEST POEMS

I know it by the number of libraries
accidents of speech
life in its ardour flames flinches
proof in hand
hard drive
autobiography of bone in series

a rare blue that exhausts
lips at the brink of crisis
how to say this is
biography in the text
let's let the heat penetrate
frontal and huge

in the body each time
this strong sense of belonging
to a small tribe
its luminous fragility anchored
in a future displaced
extreme tension in the joints
before the sea and its sites

out of breath and enunciation
time to throw off the black cold
of eternity
to recompose
this fullness of words in the chest
to detest winter and guns

sun and crazy sum of silence
so as to watch for times of great mourning
scars their fixed glow planted
in time like insects
obstinately turned to the sea

powerful sensation of life under the tongue
it often feels
like a dialogue
a few syllables their fertile trembling
between the eyelids at the moment of rousing
the sentence
life with its huge torso of hanging garden

in the fierce tumble of light
I constantly seek
amid old definitions
the troubling thinness of each second

blood's motion fervid full of life
story
of skin surface and *surfing*
signs of tenderness abound
fluvial mauve or bottomless colour
this morning you noticed it
drowned in the fragile blue of daybreak
blood no longer responds

fullness of flesh I always fear
to lose sight of a single day
of life in stable time
the loving timbre of your voice
abyss that clings to the vocal cords

the pool's water in changing light
no one dares cry out their vulnerability
the pages await mourning and absence
metaphors on alert
no one had seen time crack like a glacier

ANALYSIS OF A SOUND IN THE MIDDLE OF THE NIGHT

time free-falling in my arms,
I await night the midpoint of midnight
life stretches out palm tree silence
unrecognizable
in the folds of representation
I speak intimate in the open air

noise of lips of water soft
time slips between births and given names
on our cheeks the sleek idea of solitude
so alive we would have caressed it and tomorrow
upright like a new album amid mores
and the sudden sound of a book: it falls

in my sleep a palace of memory
history now soundproof
sueño along existential paths
sono along bones

in the beginning of solitudes
flesh quite electric
the word-for-word of the mind
bonne vivante I palpate
the astonishing configuration of an entire life

this is how we'll recall
museum visits long past
the sound of anguish having crossed over
novels certitudes and solitude
as if the future had doubled back

here and there tombs scattered
the sound of everything is so true
ever set down

for years the same question
while breathing in front of the map of the world
in front of the clock's tools
in bone territory under the moon
then out of nowhere
this sudden silence born of a drop of water
like a *do you remember*
mobile above the head
a crazy silence
in sight of desire and of our organs laid out

cold once more has taken shape
India and its rivers mow down
our self-satisfied rest
our leaden human matter
transposed
night tree in digital flower
all image of night depleted
because of the words that prepared it
in the midst of eyelashes

night veers with its leaves of green ink
quiet
I'm going to the edge of the abyss
look for me by the river
tell me I'm incapable of wounds
each phrase treads blue *à la limite*

all my limbs of pleasure and slow planet
their vibration in the green wind
all my limbs of pleasure
flattened in an uneven dream
where pain and desire make humidity
shade
and perfection out of Fridays in July

THE THROAT OF LEE MILLER

/ each time *une phrase*
opens with an I
she must be really young

and as we translate her
we must avoid saying never or in my view

I remember the throat of Lee Miller
one June day in Paris

/ often in the same phrase I return
knowing to repeat just there
where worry still craves vows entwined

and as we translate
to explain my *genre* I watch

the throat of Lee Miller that year
it was worth every abstraction

/ I often move to the same spot
a woman in love
to capture shade at the same hour

and as we translate
I breathe

the throat of Lee Miller perfection
of the image as I draw near

/ often in the midst of the phrase I am
breathless I observe
I can stay that way a long time without memory

and as we translate
I touch certain places I exhaust myself

the throat of Lee Miller
no trace of a kiss

/ above the city and the museum
huge intelligent lips signal
in a red that calls everything into question

and as we translate
I restrict myself to the top part of the work

the throat of Lee Miller around four in the afternoon
a silver-print day

/ I often said every day
art stretches out in our lives as two-
edged dialogue

and as we translate
I cross the Rue de l'Observatoire

the throat of Lee Miller in mind
lips or bodies entangled I observe

/ now in the thick of winter raging red
Geneviève Cadieux's *Milky Way*
I don't think I suffered from the comparison

and as we translate
bien sûr il n'y a pas de rapport

the bared throat of Lee Miller
open to speculation

THE SILENCE OF THE HIBISCUS

the soul of people I've long searched for it
in the blind spots of pleasure
and a few promises sunflowers spun
toward a better definition of pain
the soul of people occasionally I drew it
trace of great shadow play expectancy of life

we say alright
someone invents a silence
around
people remain stuck in the forenoon
we sought an idea
the past resurfaced
the sun will soon fade
rose
humanity in a footnote

someone tells a story
perhaps a woman
probably July
heat like oil on the back of the neck
someone coughs
rare words this time
a hand on her century

between someone and me
a bone spun round
whiter than the rose summer
higher than silence

I was surrounded by palm trees
a furor was moving in all prose
instinctively I pressed my belly to the night

that night she wrote
right-handed
eyes wide fixed to the glow
of midnight
thus swiftly she took hold
of dreams and bones that passed by
quietening only dawn at the far edge of her eyes

truly someone was inventing
my life by comparing it
with others as in fiction
with the heat of July

something incompatible
an intelligence full of artifice
that we've possibly mixed in with history
taking into account violence
the origin of plants
and the breadth of hope

this morning the woman navigates
between pain and someone young
in her veins time races quickly
rushing to encroach on the present

later as if it were better
to draw close to the stars
eyes fixed on the rare and unexpected colour
born of the meeting of pain and electricity
the woman always ready to seize life
without turning round

at the seashore and beneath the palms. The days.
Tomorrow extends our brief story. We
breathe at the heart of a punctuation that revives
a generation here, a river, a war. Over there
the young and beautiful collections of colts, nintendo,
syringes.
Logos, *loco*, forgotten lectrice.
Tonight the woman. Tonight someone.
Then there'll be just one bed
for the war and the river

as if pain such a vital organ could
produce by itself alone
the finest spectacles of la solitude humaine
and nights by the hundreds tasting of salt and sex

she said watching the approach of
the millennium and someone in her difference
intense always *live*
we lapse into forgetting
our hand galloping over a skull

when life feeds itself
as it goes along
on bones and archives undoing all chronology
I cling to every episode
where the hand fills
with salt and sand and elsewhere

The woman knew the taste of margaritas
salt that rolls grain by grain on the lip.
In the sun, time and pain formed a logical blur.
Red. With unlimited nuances.
Deliberately you let yourself be
seduced while changing ornaments on your body.

something incompatible
with suffering
a joy only fiction can launch anew
delirium that clings to every calendar

the woman said caressing
una copa de leche
agora polis ipso facto
the other responded
Je vais encore au cinéma
The woman ran a hand
across the back of her neck.
Ipso facto I pressed my belly to hers

Someone spoke at last. Of suffering
and a little dust.
Beneath a palm tree a child.
She grabbed her mother as if onto a collective
intelligence. A glass of milk in hand.
The furor of love grew.
I replied only *travaux en cours*
if someone ventured
up to her neck in the sea

I don't like when people say
one to mean someone
just hearing the voice
that said it
the throat filled with sobs
a hand on her century
knife on the words

people lived with their dead
with portraits ideas about collision
everyone wanted out
free of marginality
the beauty of gardens. Someone

the parrots the iguanas
the woman caressed them long enough for a photo
childhood and lens commingled
in the far-off colour of a first alphabet

she says she had been useful
more than once taking vertigo
as a vital aspect of intimacy
just like the body
surprised in intense moments of pleasure

The woman had run her hand through my life.
Caressing a prior world
I said timing sonorous alright.
Someone invents a silence
in our very nature.
In the morning, the love of contradictions leaves us
in terrible excitement. Pages brimming humidity
out the window. Palm trees.
All subjectivity at grips with language held in respect.
In the distance, the day sets in shades of ink and
incremental.

Now someone walked between palm trees
the ones that let silence pass easily
between their leaves.
I still don't know how long
skulls endure the fervour of centuries
of exhibition in white museums.

I don't know if it's neck-deep in the sea
that life reclaims from the night these images
of pleasure and high tides
able to haunt us
through all these centuries of beauty.

NICOLE BROSSARD's collections of poetry have twice won the Governor General's Literary Award and the Grand Prix de la poésie de la Fondation des Forges. She has been honoured with the Lifetime Recognition Award from the Griffin Trust for Excellence in Poetry, the Canada Council for the Arts Molson Prize, the Prix Athanase David, the inaugural Blue Metropolis Violet Prize, and the Harbourfront Festival Prize, among other awards, and her work has been translated into ten languages. She is an officer of the Order of Canada, chevalière of the National Order of Quebec, and a member of l'Académie des lettres du Québec. In addition to her poetry, Brossard has written novels, plays, and essays; directed two films; and co-founded the literary journal *La Barre du Jour*. She lives in Montreal.

ROBERT MAJZELS won the Governor General's Literary Award for his translation of France Daigle's novel *Just Fine*, and he has been nominated for the Griffin Poetry Prize, the Governor General's Literary Award, and the Best Translated Book Award for his translations (with Erín Moure) of Nicole Brossard's poetry. He taught English and Creative Writing at the University of Calgary from 2006 to 2013.

One of Canada's most respected poets, ERÍN MOURE is a translator and co-translator of poetry from French, Spanish, Galician, and Portuguese, and the author of 18 books of poetry, a coauthored book of poetry, a volume of essays, a book of articles on translation, a biopoetics, and two memoirs.

The A List

The Outlander Gil Adamson
The Circle Game Margaret Atwood
Moving Targets Margaret Atwood
Power Politics Margaret Atwood
Second Words Margaret Atwood
Survival Margaret Atwood
These Festive Nights Marie-Claire Blais
Thunder and Light Marie-Claire Blais
La Guerre Trilogy Roch Carrier
The Hockey Sweater and Other Stories Roch Carrier
When He Was Free and Young and He Used to Wear Silks Austin Clarke
Columbus and the Fat Lady and Other Stories Matt Cohen
Hard Core Logo Nick Craine
Great Expectations Edited by Dede Crane and Lisa Moore
Queen Rat Lynn Crosbie
The Honeyman Festival Marian Engel
The Bush Garden Northrop Frye
Eleven Canadian Novelists Interviewed by Graeme Gibson
Five Legs Graeme Gibson
Death Goes Better with Coca-Cola Dave Godfrey
Technology and Empire George Grant
Technology and Justice George Grant
De Niro's Game Rawi Hage
Kamouraska Anne Hébert
Ticknor Sheila Heti
Waterloo Express Paulette Jiles
No Pain Like This Body Harold Sonny Ladoo
Red Diaper Baby James Laxer
Civil Elegies Dennis Lee
Mermaids and Ikons Gwendolyn MacEwen
Ana Historic Daphne Marlatt
Like This Leo McKay Jr.
The Selected Short Fiction of Lisa Moore
Furious Erín Moure
Selected Poems Alden Nowlan
Poems for All the Annettes Al Purdy
Manual for Draft-Age Immigrants to Canada Mark Satin
Rochdale David Sharpe
The Little Girl Who Was Too Fond of Matches Gaétan Soucy
Stilt Jack John Thompson
Made for Happiness Jean Vanier
Basic Black with Pearls Helen Weinzweig
Passing Ceremony Helen Weinzweig
The Big Why Michael Winter
This All Happened Michael Winter